I Can't Believe It's
PARACORD
Jewelry With a Twist™

Barbara Matthiessen

Introduction

Move over simple knotted bracelets! We've taken paracord to a whole new level in this book of stunning jewelry. Designer Barbara Matthiessen teaches you how to create a wide variety of jewelry using paracord that will leave you wanting more! No longer just for the outdoor enthusiast, paracord is being used for all types of wearables, jewelry and accessories. Paracord is extremely strong and durable and comes in a wide array of colors, including multitones and even glow-in-the-dark. This book guides you through 13 amazing designs that incorporate all types of beads, chain, fabrics and fibers. From a soft-draping dyed cowl that incorporates T-shirt material with paracord to beaded jewelry, these projects are fun. Simple, step-by-step drawings and color photos make the projects easy to understand and quick to complete. So pick some colorful cord, grab your tools, and join in the fun!

Meet the Designer

Barbara Matthiessen has been creating in the Arts and Crafts industry for close to 20 years. She has designed kits, written hundreds of magazine articles, and written several books. A desire to help others be creative inspires her to discover innovative techniques and materials. Barbara lives in the beautiful Northwest and says she finds the area a constant source of inspiration for her creativity.

Contents

General Instructions

WORKING WITH PARACORD

Knotting paracord is a popular crafting activity that uses many standard macramé techniques. The diameter of paracord produces sizable knots, allowing a single or a few decorative knots to create impact. Most of the projects in this book can be knotted in your hand or on a flat surface; some projects are easier to do on a clipboard, pinned to scrap cardboard or foam board, or as with the Turks Head Bracelet, on a can or jar.

Due to its resilient nature, you may need to finesse some of your paracord knots. Simply work the knot into shape with your hands, smoothing and rotating it as needed.

When it comes to knotting with paracord, everyone has a slightly different style. Some people's knots are tight, while others' knots are loose. Cord measurements given for each project should allow you to complete the project and have a slight cushion of cord left over. In general, your cords will need to be four to five times the finished length of your project, depending on the number of knots.

> If your paracord does not melt cleanly, cover up the exposed core by using a permanent marker in a matching color.

tip

SEWING PARACORD

Thanks to the finely braided sheath, paracord can also be stitched using common sewing supplies. Using strong beading thread, Kevlar or button thread, you can turn under edges and add beads, charms or jewelry findings by stitching. Make sure to use a needle with an eye that will accommodate your thread. Stitch a knot through the sheath, leaving a thread tail to secure. If you knot your thread before starting to stitch, as is traditionally done, the knots tend to pull through the cord.

CUTTING & FINISHING ENDS

Paracord will unravel when cut. Cut the end with sharp scissors and then melt the cut end using a butane lighter. Work over a protected surface that will allow you to roll the melted end into a nice cylindrical shape. Or you can use a pair of pliers to shape the end while hot. With some brands of paracord, the inner core will melt flat and even, but others tend to bubble slightly, which can be both unsightly and hard to finish cleanly. Be careful of the melted end; it is hot and can cause a burn!

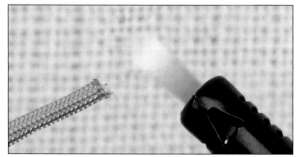

BASIC KNOTS

There are only a few knots you need to learn to be able to create stunning jewelry. These knots can be combined in endless combinations to create beautiful, original pieces that also have practical applications.

OVERHAND KNOT

This knot is often used to gather cords together, to secure a bead or as an ending. To create this knot:

1. Make a loop; bring end of cord through the loop and out.

2. Tighten.

Overhand Knot

DOUBLE OVERHAND KNOT

A Double Overhand Knot is created by tying two Overhand Knots next to each other on a piece of cord.

SQUARE KNOT

Square Knots are used to create bands, add decorative accents and to secure cords and other materials. Tightened down, this is a very secure knot. Most commonly done with four cords—two core cords and two working cords—it can also be done over a group of cords. To create this knot:

1. Fold one length of cord in half to locate center. These will be the core cords. Measure one inch down from top of loop and mark with a pin. Secure loop to top of a clipboard or pin to foam or cardboard working surface. Fold another length of cord in half to find its center. These cord ends will be the working left-hand

and working right-hand cords (the outer cords). Place the center of this cord under the core cords, one inch down from the top of the loop as marked by the pin. ***Note:*** *If using foam or cardboard, pin center of working cord in place if desired.*

2. Fold the right-hand end of the outer cord over the core cords to create a loop that looks like the bottom of the letter b. Thread the left-hand end of the outer cord over the tail of the loop, under core cords, and out through the loop of "b." Pull equally on each tail to tighten; slide knot to the 1-inch mark as needed. This completes the first half of the square knot.

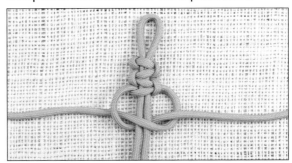

3. For the second half of knot, fold the left-hand end of the outer cord over core cords to create a loop that looks like the bottom of the letter d. Thread the right-hand end of the outer cord over the tail of the loop, under core cords, and out through the loop of "d." Pull equally on each tail to tighten. This completes the square knot. Repeat as instructed for each project.

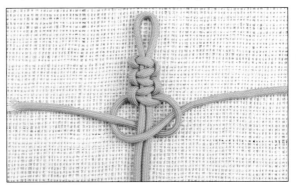

GATHERING KNOT

This knot is often used to end a piece or to secure one end to another by tightly wrapping around a group of cords. To create this knot:

1. Fold a loop of cord on top of the cords that will be gathered, adjusting the cord so that one tail is longer than the other. This longer tail will be your working end.

2. With the working end of the looped cord, start tightly wrapping up, over and around the gathered cords and looped cord moving toward the folded loop. *Note: The end of the loop cord being wrapped is the working end of the cord.* Wrap tightly, keeping coils next to each other until you reach the top of the loop.

3. Insert the working end of cord through the loop, then pull the short/secured cord tail on the opposite end. The loop and the working end will be pulled inside the knot and secured. Trim off cord tails as needed.

SIMPLE BRAID

Braids have been used for decorative purposes throughout history. The simplest three-strand braids can fit any style you desire simply by choice of materials. To create a three-strand braid:

1. Begin with three cords. Fold the right-hand cord over the center cord. This is now your new center cord. Fold the left-hand cord over the center cord. This is now your new center cord.

2. Continue to alternate folding the right- and left-hand cords over the center cord until desired braid length is reached.

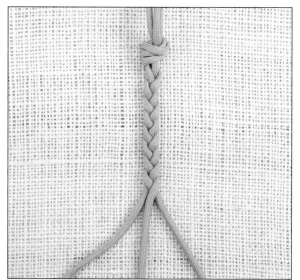

To complete some of the designs in this book, you will need some basic jewelry tools.

Chain-Nose Pliers are the most useful tool in your entire toolbox. They are used for holding, opening and closing jump rings, and bending sharp angles.

Round-Nose Pliers are intended for turning round loops. They do not work well for holding or grasping since they tend to leave a small dent.

Flat-Nose Pliers are a wire power tool. They are excellent for turning sharp corners, holding items, and for opening and closing jump rings.

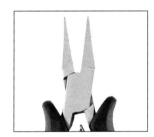

Wire Flush Cutters leave one flat side and one pointed side on each cut. Using flush cutters is especially important when working with heavy gauges of wire

(20-gauge or smaller). One side of the cutter is flat, and the other is indented. ***Note:*** *Cutting any type of chain with your scissors will damage the scissors.*

OPENING & CLOSING A SIMPLE LOOP OR JUMP RING

1. Use two pairs of chain-nose pliers. Push ring open with right pliers while holding across the ring with left pliers.

2. To close, hold in the same way and rock the ring back and forth until ring ends rub against each other or you hear a click. Moving the ring past the closed position and then back hardens the ring and ensures a tight closure.

3. To open a loop, use a pair of chain-nose pliers to twist the loop open. Twist to close, making sure the opening in the loop is tightly closed.

SIMPLE LOOP

1. Bend the wire 90 degrees just above bead. Trim excess to ¼ inch.

2. Grasp end with round-nose pliers and roll into loop.

3. Readjust position of tool to finish the loop, if needed.

4. Adjust loop as necessary.

WRAPPED WIRE LOOPS

1. String beads onto head pin or eye pin.

2. Grasp wire above beads with round-nose pliers. Bend wire to 90-degree angle over top of pliers.

3. Place pliers above bend. Pull wire around until it crosses in front of itself, forming a loop.

4. Place round-nose pliers into loop; wrap wire tail around the wire stem until space between loop and beads is wrapped with wire.

5. Trim wire as close to coil as possible; press end down with pliers.

tip

Using the proper tools and techniques when making jewelry can enhance the quality of the finished piece.

WORKING WITH CHAINS

Often you will need to shorten a length of chain. Ball chain and other very fine chains can be cut to length using wire cutters. To shorten larger chains with open links, open the link just past the link that will give you the appropriate length of chain using the Opening & Closing a Simple Loop or Jump Ring method. Individual chain links can be used like jump rings to attach findings and give your piece a cohesive look.

If your chain has solid links or is linked with wraps, you will need to cut away a link to create desired lengths.

CLOSURES

A number of types of closures are possible with paracord. The Sliding Knot is a popular choice and is suited to many of the projects in this book. Other closure methods include Loop & Button, adding traditional jewelry findings such as clasps or toggles, or finishing with cord caps and findings.

LOOP & BUTTON

You will need: ½ inch or larger bead or button, thread, sewing needle and a pin. Fold a loop on one side or end; pin in place. Test-fit button or bead. Stitch base of loop then attach bead or button to other side/end.

ADDING TRADITIONAL FINDINGS

Traditional clasps can either be stitched directly to paracord ends or attached with jump rings. Pass paracord through jump ring then back down on itself; by doing this you make sure the cord will fit through the ring. Stitch into place.

CORD TIPS & COILS

Cord tips and coils can be glued on or glued and crimped on depending on the style. Follow the manufacturer's instructions, and then add findings of your choice, attaching through loops of cord tips or coils.

SLIDING KNOTS

Sliding knots make great simple closures that allow adjustment of necklace length. You can substitute these knots for any necklace closure in this book.

SINGLE KNOT SLIDER

Cross ends so they are pointing opposite directions. Fold top cord back 8 inches, forming a loop on top of bottom cord. Hold cords securely while you wrap top cord tail away from loop and around both cords four times. Do not wrap tightly.

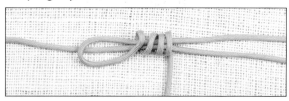

Thread end of wrapping cord back through wraps you just made, moving up toward the folded loop end. Pull on ends, easing knot tighter and tighter. Finesse knot and cords until they are smooth and secure. Tie overhand knots on cord ends; trim and melt.

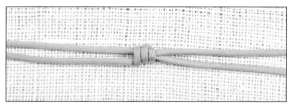

DOUBLE KNOT SLIDER

Cross ends so they are pointing in opposite directions. On one side, wrap cord end around the opposite cord; tie an overhand knot. Repeat on opposite side. ●

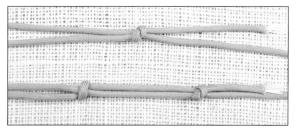

Easy Does It

WRIST MEASUREMENT FOR CORD LENGTHS

CORE CORD FORMULA

Measure your wrist. Add 1–2 inches to this measurement. Double this measurement and add 6 inches. This will be the measurement for your core cord. Example formula for core cord with a 7-inch wrist measurement:

7-inch (wrist) + 2 inches = 9 inches

9 inches x 2 = 18 inches

18 inches + 6 inches = 24 inches

Core cord length for a 7-inch wrist will be 24 inches.

OUTER CORD FORMULA

For outer cord measurement, multiply the core cord measurement by three. **Note:** *Having a little extra cord makes finishing the ends easier.* Example formula for outer cord using a 7-inch wrist core cord measurement:

24-inch (core cord) x 3 = 72 inches

Outer cord length for a 7-inch wrist will be 72 inches.

Total amount of paracord needed for a 7-inch wrist (core cord + outer cord): 96 inches.

MATERIALS
Paracord in
   desired color*
Sharp scissors
Marker
Straight pin
Ruler
Butane lighter
Clipboard, cardboard or
   foam board

Use measurement gained from Wrist Measurement for Cord Lengths section to determine the amount of paracord need.

FINISHED SIZE
Varies by wrist size.

INSTRUCTIONS

Project note: *After cutting, melt ends of paracord using a lighter. Materials and colors used are to aid in photography instructions and may not match finished project.*

1. Cut one core cord and one outer cord from paracord according to length formulas.

2. Fold core cord in half. Measure 1 inch down from the fold and place a straight pin at mark. Pin the top of the loop to foam or cardboard, or place loop under clip on clipboard (Figure 1).

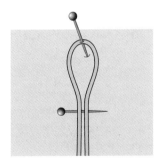

Figure 1

3. Fold outer cord in half to locate center. Place center of outer cord under core cords at 1-inch mark. Begin creating a Square Knot (page 5) by folding the right-hand end of outer cord over core cords to create a loop that looks like the bottom of the letter b. Thread the left-hand end of outer cord over the tail of the loop, under core cords, and out through the loop of the "b." Pull equally on each tail to tighten. Remove pin and slide knot to 1-inch mark.

4. Finish Square Knot by folding the left-hand end of outer cord over core cords to create a loop that looks like the bottom of the letter d. Thread the right-hand end of outer cord over the tail of the loop, under core cords, and out through the loop of the "d." Pull equally on each tail to tighten.

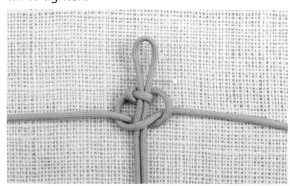

Repeating a simple square knot can create a chunky bracelet with great texture. Try using different colors of paracord to add even more interest to this design!

tip

5. Repeat steps 3 and 4 until your bracelet is the desired length.

6. Tie four ends of cords in an Overhand Knot (page 5) to finish bracelet. Test to ensure loop fits over knot. If bracelet is desired size, pull Overhand Knot to tighten. If bracelet size needs adjustment, remove Overhand Knot and add or remove Square Knots to adjust size. Re-tie Overhand Knot. Pull to tighten. Trim and melt ends to complete. ●

Color Me Blue

MATERIALS

¾ yard white, lightweight
   jersey fabric 60 inches
   wide cut into:
   7 (3 x 60-inch) strips
White paracord:
   1 (8-foot), 8 (4½-foot),
   1 (12-inch)
Liquid dye for nylon in
   preferred color

Rubber band
Sharp scissors
Butane lighter
Ruler

FINISHED SIZE

Approximately 36 inches

INSTRUCTIONS

Project note: *After cutting, melt ends of paracord using lighter. Materials and colors used are to aid in photography instructions and may not match finished project.*

1. Gather one end of each seven pieces of jersey fabric and eight pieces of 4½-foot-long paracord, alternating fabric and cord. ***Note:*** *Fabric will be longer than paracord.* Temporarily hold together by wrapping rubber band around gathered pieces 1 inch from end. Trim fabric at slight angle to reduce bulk. Reposition rubber band to cover entire end.

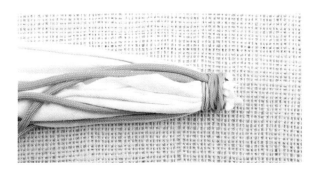

2. Loop length around neck, overlapping ends and allowing 18 inches to hang past the rubber band. Using a 12-inch piece of paracord, tie an Overhand Knot (page 5) around overlapping pieces at rubber band (Figure 1).

Figure 1

3. Use the 8-foot piece of paracord to tie a Gathering Knot (page 6) on top of the overlapped fabric. To help disguise the cut ends of fabric and cord, position the rubber band area in the center of the fabric strips.

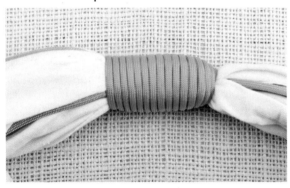

4. Pull two hanging jersey strips, one from each side. Tie four Square Knots (page 5) over and around fabric strips and paracord. Tighten all knots.

5. Try necklace on and trim loose jersey and paracord ends as desired. You may trim to all one length or to varied lengths. Melt trimmed paracord ends.

6. Dye finished necklace with liquid dye following manufacturer's directions. ●

Turks Head
Bracelet

INSTRUCTIONS

Project note: *After cutting, melt ends of paracord using lighter. Materials and colors used are to aid in photography instructions and may not match finished project.*

1. Tape one end of paracord to can to secure. Wrap cord around the can and over itself, forming an X. **Note:** *Don't wrap too tightly or you won't be able to complete the weaving process.*

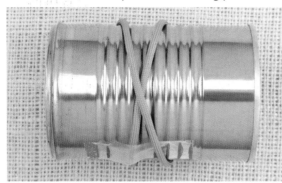

MATERIALS	Jar, can or cardboard
14 feet paracord in	tube sized to fit
desired color	overhand (Measure
Sewing thread	around hand with
Sewing needle	fingers cupped
Sharp scissors	together then
Butane lighter	add 1 inch.)
Ruler	Tape
Tweezers or needle-nose	
pliers (optional)	**FINISHED SIZE**
	Approximately 7½ inches

2. Wrap cord around can again, bringing the cord up and over the center of the X from step 1.

3. Thread the cord under the right-hand cord just after the X. Pull the remaining length of cord through.

4. Push the left-hand cord up and over the right-hand cord. The two cords now cross, creating an eye shape.

5. Thread the cord end under the newly created left-hand cord and pull all the way through.

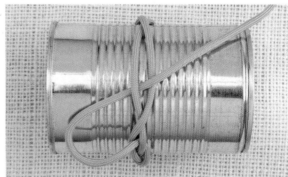

6. Pull the X of the two crossing cords down, creating a braid-like appearance.

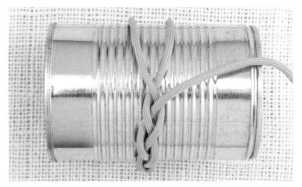

7. Repeat steps 3–6 until you get about 2 inches from the beginning point. If needed, force cords into place to appear as they do in photo. Remove tape from first end of cord; pull cord end through center and out to right as shown. Tape down.

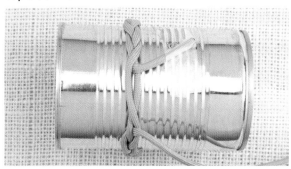

8. Continue weaving as before until the cord comes up through the same eye-shaped hole as the original tail that is taped to the right.

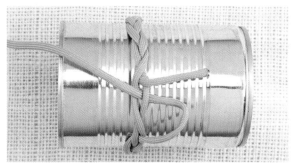

9. Carefully remove the bracelet from the can. Put a piece of tape around the short right-hand tail so it does not easily pull out of the weaving while you continue the bracelet.

10. With the long cord, follow the first-round cord, weaving over and under in the same pattern. Continue for a third round. ***Note:*** *As you get closer to the original weaving point, the cord will become tighter. You may need to use tweezers or a pair of needle-nose pliers to weave your cord.*

11. When finished, thread cord ends to inside of bracelet. Trim to ½ inch then melt ends. Stitch to inside cords of bracelet to secure. ●

tip

Many people find it is easier to tie this knot without a cylinder and instead hold it in their hands. If you do use a cylinder, don't wrap too tightly or it will be difficult to weave. If using a can, file down sharp edges. Think of doing a simple three-cord braid while creating this bracelet. If you get confused during the first round, decide where a cord would go if doing a braid.

Better Than Pearls

INSTRUCTIONS

Project note: Only melt ends of paracord after cutting, using lighter when instructed to. Materials and colors used are to aid in photography instructions and may not match finished project.

MATERIALS

White paracord (Do
   not melt ends after
   cutting.): 3 (14-inch),
   1 (36-inch)
Clear faceted beads:
   4 (14mm) round, 3
   (6mm), 2 (18 x 14mm)
   rondelles, 2 (16 x
   12mm) rondelles,
   1 (23mm) cluster bead
2 (5mm) round metal
   silver beads
2 (23mm) round cluster
   pearl beads
2 (11 x 5mm) silver
   metal rondelles
2 (18mm) round cluster
   pearl beads
2 (12 x 9mm)
   white opaque
   faceted rondelles

2 (21 x 17mm)
   silver bead caps
1 (12 x 20mm) silver disc
   bead or decorative
   button with shank
No. 6 white silk
   beading thread
White heavy-weight
   sewing thread
Safety pins
Beading mat or beading
   board (optional)
Sewing needle
   with large eye
Jewelry adhesive
Sharp scissors
Butane lighter
Ruler

FINISHED SIZE
26 inches, including clasp

---

1. Pull the center cores out of each 14-inch piece of white paracord. **Note:** If your white paracord happens to have a colored string in the core, you can remove just that string or you can keep it for added interest.

2. Tie an Overhand Knot (page 5) close to ends to secure strings of center cores. Set aside.

3. Fold 36-inch paracord in half to locate center. At center of cord, tie a Double Overhand Knot (page 5).

4. Measure 4 inches from center knot and tie Double Overhand Knot. Repeat for other side of center knot.

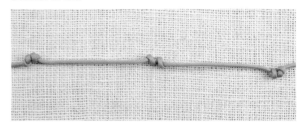

5. Measure 1½ inches from last knot on each side of paracord. Mark with a safety pin. Lay center string cores from step 1 beside knotted paracord. Line up the knots on string cores with the safety pins. There should be some slack in the string cores to create the whimsical look of the necklace. Adjust pins as needed to create desired look.

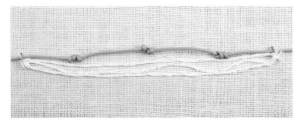

6. Use sturdy sewing thread and needle to stitch knots of string cores to paracord outer sheath. Stagger the knots, keeping them in a small area that will be covered by the bead cap.

7. Lay beads in desired pattern on beading mat or beading board.

8. Thread beading thread through large eye of sewing needle. ***Note:*** *Make sure threaded needle will fit through hole in beads.* Stitch through area where string core knots are attached to paracord sheath. Knot and secure beading thread. Add a drop of jewelry adhesive to knot. String beads on prepared needle, and then stitch beaded strand to corresponding spot on opposite side. Stitch multiple times and tie knot. Add a drop of jewelry adhesive over knot and stitches.

9. Thread bead caps onto paracord ends and down over knots. Tie an Overhand Knot to secure bead cap tight to knots.

tip

A Double Overhand Knot is created by tying two Overhand Knots next to each other on a piece of cord.

10. On one side of necklace, tie an Overhand Knot 2 inches from knot beside bead cap. Tie another Overhand Knot 3 inches from last knot created. Repeat on opposite side of necklace.

11. Fold one end of paracord back 1½ inches. Secure in place using a safety pin. Test to make sure loop will slide over bead or button closure. Adjust size if necessary. Stitch end down (Figure 1).

12. Thread sewing needle with heavy-weight sewing thread. Knot end to form double thread. Fold unfinished side of necklace over ½ inch. Stitch securely but do not cut thread. Thread disc bead and 6mm faceted round clear bead onto thread. Stitch back through metal disc bead and cord. Repeat 2–3 times, stitching through disc, faceted bead and paracord. Knot thread and dot with glue to secure (Figure 2). ●

Figure 1

Figure 2

Wild About Knots

NECKLACE MATERIALS

9 feet paracord in
    desired color
22-inch length 10 x
    14mm oval link chain
2 (7 x 13mm) cord
    end findings
13 (15mm) jump rings
Large clasp
Scrap cardboard or
    foam board

Straight pins
Safety pins
Chain-nose pliers
Sharp scissors
Butane lighter
Ruler
Jewelry adhesive

FINISHED SIZE

Approximately 26 inches,
    including clasp

NECKLACE

INSTRUCTIONS

Project note: *After cutting, melt ends of paracord using lighter. Materials and colors used are to aid in photography instructions and may not match finished project. Use straight pins to secure loops of paracord in place as needed.*

1. Measure 4 inches from left-hand end of cord. Place safety pin. The right-hand end will be your working end.

2. To make a Josephine Knot, first create a clockwise loop next to the safety pin with the working end over the left-hand tail.

3. Create a second clockwise loop over the top of the first loop. Thread the working end under the left-hand tail.

4. Thread the working end over left edge of top loop and under left edge of bottom loop.

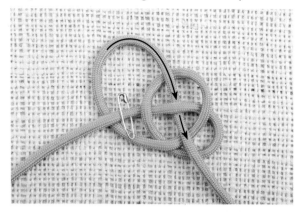

5. Thread the working end over right edge of top loop and under right edge of bottom loop. Adjust knot size to approximately 1½ inches wide.

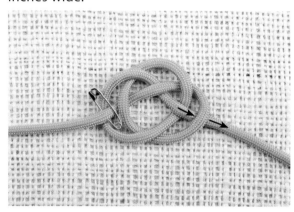

6. Repeat steps 2–5 nine more times for a total of 10 Josephine Knots. Adjust each knot as needed and space knots ¾ inch apart. Place a few discrete stitches on the back side of each knot at the stress points to help your knots keep their shape and size.

7. Tie Overhand Knot (page 5) on each end 1 inch from Josephine Knots.

8. Lay Josephine Knots out in straight line. Lay chain next to knots. Open a jump ring. Thread jump ring onto end link of chain. Attach to cord between Overhand Knot and first Josephine Knot. Close jump ring. Open another jump ring. Thread jump ring onto link six of chain and cord between first and second Josephine Knots. *Note: Number of links of chain between jump rings will depend on size of chain. Adjust link count as necessary for chain to lie evenly around knots.* Continue to attach chain to paracord between Josephine Knots until other end of necklace has been reached. Remove extra links of chain. Attach jump ring to last link of chain and to cord between last Josephine Knot and Overhand Knot.

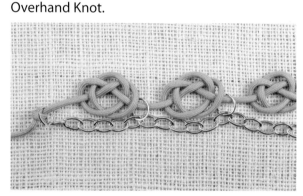

9. Attach cord end finding according to manufacturer's directions.

10. Use jump rings to attach clasp finding to each cord end.

> **tip**
>
> Finished length of this necklace and bracelet will be affected by the size and tightness of the knots along with the measurement between knots.

BRACELET MATERIALS	Safety pins
4 feet paracord in desired color	Sharp scissors
	Butane lighter
½-inch decorative shank button	Ruler
Sewing thread	**FINISHED SIZE**
Needle	Varies by wrist size.

BRACELET

INSTRUCTIONS

Project note: *After cutting, melt ends of paracord using lighter. Materials and colors used are to aid in photography instructions and may not match finished project.*

1. Fold cord in half. Tie an Overhand Knot (page 5) about 1 inch from the folded end. Test to make sure the loop will fit over your button. Adjust as needed.

2. Measure 2½ inches from Overhand Knot and place a safety pin to secure two cords together.

3. Tie a Josephine Knot at edge of safety pin, following steps 2–5 from Wild About Knots Necklace instructions and treating the two cords as one. Adjust cords so they lie flat throughout the knot.

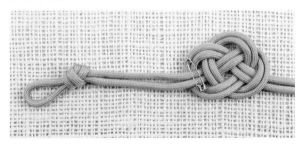

4. Measure 2½ inches past Josephine Knot and place safety pin through both cords. Thread shank button onto safety pin. Test-fit bracelet. Adjust pin and button as needed. Trim and melt ends of cord. Stitch button securely to end of two cords. ●

Lovely Loops

INSTRUCTIONS

Project note: *After cutting, melt ends of paracord using lighter. Materials and colors used are to aid in photography instructions and may not match finished project.*

1. Lay cord between your thumb and first finger with the short tail sticking out behind your hand.

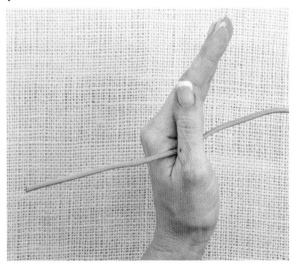

MATERIALS	
16 feet paracord in desired color	Sharp scissors
	Butane lighter
18-inch length of chain with links large enough to slide over paracord	Ruler
	Jewelry adhesive
24 x 1-inch torn fabric strip	**FINISHED SIZE**
	Approximately 31 inches

2. With the long working end of the cord, wrap cord around front of first finger and weave back and forth between the rest of the fingers. Wrap around little finger and weave between fingers going back the other direction. Wrap cord around your first finger again and repeat process of wrapping until you have two loops around each finger.

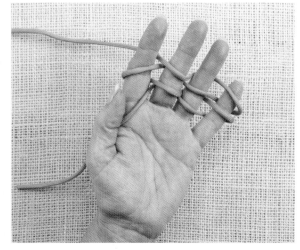

3. Pull the cord around your first finger and down onto your palm. Secure with your thumb.

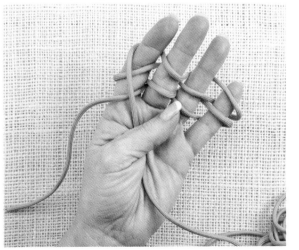

4. Starting with your little finger, pull the bottom cord up over the top cord and let it fall behind your finger. Continue for the next two fingers. When you get to your first finger, the bottom cord will be the short tail that you started with. Pull that tail and place it through your first and second fingers, leaving the tail hang down the back of your hand.

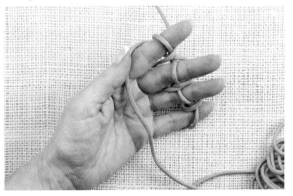

5. Bring the working cord around the front of your first finger and again weave through and back through all fingers, keeping the new loops at the top of your fingers. Pull working cord around to palm to secure with thumb. Starting with little finger, loop bottom cord over top cord and let drop down behind hand. Continue pulling bottom loops up over top loops for all fingers. This will form a ladder-looking weave that hangs down the back of your hand.

6. Repeat step 5 until remaining working cord is approximately 18 inches long.

7. To remove weaving, take loop from little finger and place over ring finger. Pull bottom loop on ring finger up and over top loop.

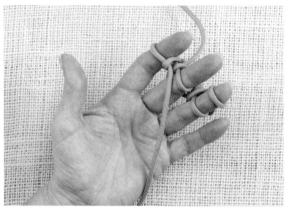

8. Repeat step 7 two more times until you have one loop on your first finger. Remove loop from first finger and thread working end of cord through loop. Pull to tighten.

9. You can leave your weaving open and loose, or you can pull on each end and create a tube-like shape.

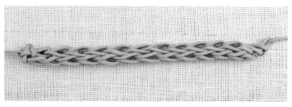

10. Insert cord ends through end links in chain. Tie an Overhand Knot (page 5). Trim and melt cord ends. Place a drop of glue on Overhand Knot or stitch to secure.

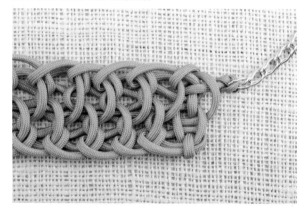

11. Tie ribbon or fabric strip over knot at chain on one side. Weave through loops as desired. Tie around knot on opposite side. Secure ribbon with a few stitches. ●

Why Knot

INSTRUCTIONS

Project note: *After cutting, melt ends of paracord using lighter. Materials and colors used are to aid in photography instructions and may not match finished project.*

1. Lay focal bead in center of beading mat or beading board. Arrange beads on both sides of focal bead, matching pattern from side to side. Reserve two large-hole rondelles for later use (Figure 1).

Figure 1

2. String and center focal bead onto wire. Fold wire around sides of bead. Twist two times above center of bead. Open wire into a "Y" shape (Figure 2).

Figure 2

3. String beads onto one side of wire. String a bead cap onto wire with large end cupping beads. Create a Wrapped Wire Loop (page 8) on end of wire as shown. Make sure the wrapped loop is large enough to accommodate the paracord. Repeat on opposite side.

4. Thread ¼ inch of one end of 17-inch paracord through wire loop; fold and stitch to secure, keeping cord as flat as possible. Repeat for opposite side.

MATERIALS	
2 (17-inch) paracord*	14 inches 16-gauge wire
18mm round focal bead*	Beading mat or beading
Rondelles*: 2 (12 x 8mm)	board (optional)
facetted glass, 2 (13	Sewing thread to
x 4mm) gold-color,	match paracord
2 (10 x 14mm) large-	Sewing needle
hole acrylic	Flush wire cutters
2 (13mm) black/	Round-nose pliers
silver decorative	Sharp scissors
round beads	Butane lighter
2 (19mm) glass	*In desired colors.
square beads*	
2 (10 x 14mm)	**FINISHED SIZE**
antiqued brass bead	Approximately 26 inches
cap findings	

5. String large-hole bead down to stitched area. Tie an Overhand Knot (page 5) next to large-hole bead. Repeat for opposite side.

6. Tie desired Sliding Knot (page 9) to join cords.

7. Tie an Overhand Knot in ends of cord tails. ●

Make sure the holes in your beads are large enough to easily slide onto the paracord.

tip

Para Pins

INSTRUCTIONS

Project note: *After cutting, melt ends of paracord using lighter. Materials and colors used are to aid in photography instructions and may not match finished project.*

1. Lay ruler and paracord on a flat surface. Using fine-tip marker, measure and mark at 3 inches and 3½ inches. Move last mark to zero on your ruler and repeat markings 11 more times for a total of 12 (3-inch) outer petals.

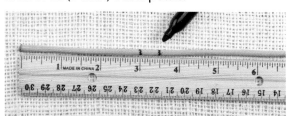

2. Beginning at your last mark from step 1, mark at 2 inches and 2½ inches. Repeat nine more times, skipping the last 2½-inch mark for a total of 10 (2-inch) inner petals.

3. Make a stitch at the end of the cord for the outer petals. Fold the cord, matching the end and the first mark, creating a petal. Stitch through cord, back through previous cord, and forward again to secure. Fold the cord again, matching next marks. Stitch to secure. Continue through large and then small petals. Stitch a knot to secure at end of petals.

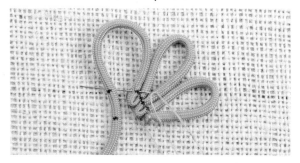

4. Coil petals into a circle starting with the smaller, inner petals. Stitch to secure. Continue to coil, keeping larger petals behind smaller petals. Stitch as needed to secure top layer of petals to bottom layer.

5. Stitch button to flower center, securing on opposite sides of the lower layer of petals to keep button centered. *Note: If desired, jewelry adhesive may be used to adhere stacked buttons to center of flower.*

6. Stitch pin back to flower back. ●

Try using an old brooch or other costume jewelry for the center of the flower.

Celtic Knot

INSTRUCTIONS

Project note: *After cutting, melt ends of paracord using lighter. Materials and colors used are to aid in photography instructions and may not match finished project.*

MATERIALS
6 feet paracord in
   desired color
2 (8-inch) lengths of
   chain in desired color
2 (2-inch) headpins to
   match chain
2 (10 x 14mm)
   metal bead caps
2 (6mm) jump rings
Lobster clasp

Coordinating or
   monofilament thread
Sewing needle
Straight pins
Round-nose pliers
Sharp scissors
Foam board or cardboard
Butane lighter

FINISHED SIZE
22 inches, including clasp

1. Fold paracord in half to create a loop (Loop 1) about the size of a quarter. Attach loop to foam or cardboard with pins. ***Note:*** *Pin following loops in the same manner, as needed.*

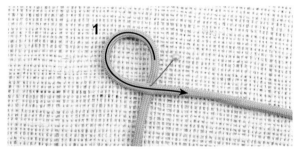

2. Referring to photo, use the top cord from Loop 1 to create a second loop (Loop 2), being careful to note the direction and placement of cords.

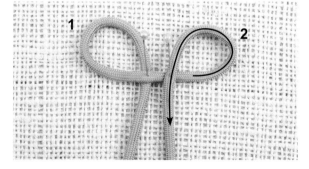

3. Create a third loop directly below Loop 2 (Loop 3). Weave the tail of Loop 3 under the tail of Loop 1.

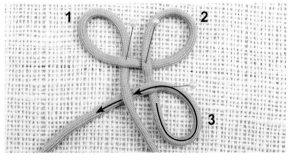

4. Lay the tail of Loop 3 over the top of Loop 1.

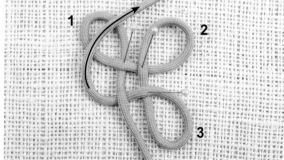

7. Thread the same tail up through the hole beside Loop 3, down through Loop 3, under the cord, and back up through Loop 3.

5. Thread the tail from Loop 1 under Loop 3, under Loop 2 and up through Loop 1, over the cord crossing the loop, and back down through loop. This tail is one side of your necklace. Secure it down with a pin.

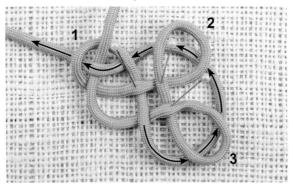

8. Remove pins and adjust knot to a triangular shape. This completes the Celtic Knot.

6. Thread the tail from Loop 3 under the cord and up through the hole between Loop 1 and Loop 2, down through Loop 2, under the cord, and back up through Loop 2.

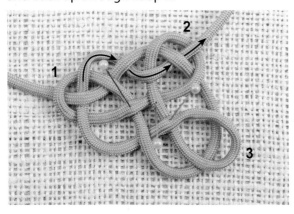

9. To keep knot shape from deteriorating when necklace is worn, place a few discrete stitches using matching color or monofilament thread on the back at stress points and cord crossing points. Secure corners with stitches to keep knot shape and size.

10. Knot ends of paracord about ½ inch away from Celtic Knot on each side of necklace using an Overhand Knot (page 5). ***Note:*** *Tie your knot so the ends lay in an upward position. This will make your necklace hang correctly.* Trim, leaving about ¼ inch past knot. Melt ends.

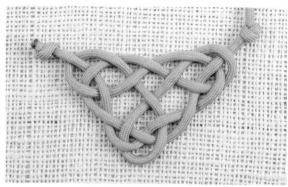

11. Insert a headpin through the knot and out through melted end. Tug on pin to make sure it is secure. If pin pulls through, reinsert in a different area and test again. ***Note:*** *It can be hard to work the pin through the cord. Use a blunt needle or a toothpick to help create a space for the headpin if needed.* Place bead cap on headpin, large end toward knot. Using round-nose pliers, form a Simple Loop (page 7) above the bead cap. Repeat for other side of necklace.

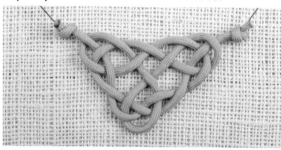

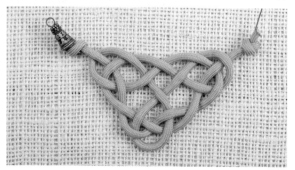

12. Open Simple Loop on one end of necklace and string on end of one piece of chain. Close loop. Repeat for other side of necklace.

13. Open and attach one jump ring to one side of chain. Use second jump ring to attach lobster clasp to other chain end. ●

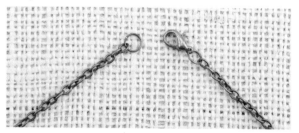

Free to Be Me

MATERIALS

Paracord: 1 (32-inch) black, 2 (32-inch) brown/tan

2 (32-inch) lengths medium-weight brass-color chain

Recycled silk yarn in desired color: 2 (9-foot), 4 (32-inch), 6 (12-inch)

Desired metal pieces for pendant: 3 skeleton keys, 2 gears

2 rubber bands

Sharp scissors

Butane lighter

Ruler

Binder clip (optional)

Clipboard (optional)

Jewelry adhesive

FINISHED SIZE

Approximately 26 inches

INSTRUCTIONS

Project note: After cutting, melt ends of paracord using lighter. Materials and colors used are to aid in photography instructions and may not match finished project. Thickness of recycled silk yarn can vary; adjust length measurements as needed.

1. Gather one end of each 32-inch length of paracord, chain and yarn pieces together. Wrap securely with a rubber band about 1 inch from one end. Secure end under clipboard if desired.

2. Divide long tail into three sections, mixing cord, yarn and chain. Create a Simple Braid (page 6) with three sections as shown. Braid until 10 inches have been braided. Place a binder clip at the end of braiding to secure.

3. String pendant pieces onto one of the brown paracord lengths, leaving a loop about 1½ inches long.

4. Remove binder clip and resume braiding to end of cords.

5. Place rubber band around end of braiding to secure.

6. Apply jewelry adhesive to all yarn and paracord strands and adhere together. Pull rubber band down over glue to secure. Repeat for opposite end. Allow glue to dry completely.

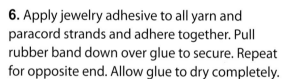

7. Carefully remove rubber band from each end of necklace. Overlap ends 1 inch. Fold one 9-foot piece of recycled silk yarn in half, then fold in half again to obtain four strand lengths. Use folded yarn to tie a Gathering Knot (page 6) over overlapped ends.

8. Repeat step 7 on the other side of necklace an equal distance from pendant.

9. To create pendant fringe, hold six strands of 12-inch pieces of recycled silk yarn as one and tie two Overhand Knots (page 5) right above pendant. ●

Free to Be Me II

INSTRUCTIONS

Project note: *After cutting, melt ends of paracord using lighter. Materials and colors used are to aid in photography instructions and may not match finished project.*

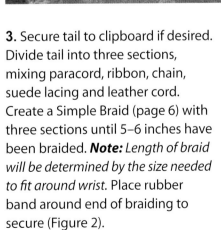

1. Thread one piece olive green paracord ½ inch through 10mm jump ring. Fold paracord and stitch flat. This will secure one end of your clasp.

2. Gather one end of each 14-inch strand of paracord, ribbon, chain, suede lacing and leather cord. Wrap ends securely with a rubber band. Allow paracord piece with jump ring attached to stick out of tail about ¼ inch (Figure 1).

Figure 1

3. Secure tail to clipboard if desired. Divide tail into three sections, mixing paracord, ribbon, chain, suede lacing and leather cord. Create a Simple Braid (page 6) with three sections until 5–6 inches have been braided. ***Note:*** *Length of braid will be determined by the size needed to fit around wrist.* Place rubber band around end of braiding to secure (Figure 2).

Figure 2

4. Test-fit bracelet to determine approximate placement of second half of clasp. Add or reduce braiding as needed for fit. Use safety pin to mark fit on one piece of cord. Open jump ring and thread on clasp, close jump ring. Thread one piece of paracord through jump ring, fold over ½ inch and pin with safety pin. Test-fit again, adjusting as necessary. Trim paracord ½ inch past jump ring. Remove jump ring and melt paracord end. Thread jump ring back onto paracord and stitch to secure.

5. Trim all other cords, ribbon and chain, being careful not to cut paracord with jump ring. Work rubber band back away from ends. Apply dots of jewelry adhesive to adhere strands together. Pull rubber band back over glued ends. Repeat glue on other end. Allow to dry completely.

tip

Achieve a whimsical look by swapping out the chain with eyelash yarn. When the bracelet is completed, gently brush the braid to loosen the eyelash yarn for a fun look.

6. Carefully remove rubber band. Use long leather cord to tie a Gathering Knot (page 6) over glued end to finish. Repeat on other end. ●

Classic Copper

MATERIALS

2 (8-foot) paracords in desired color

28 inches ½-inch-wide soft copper tubing (Extra tubing length is so you can hang on to it while cutting.)

Copper clasp

Sewing thread

Sewing needle

18-inch cardboard scrap

Straight pins

Copper pipe tube cutter

Hammer

Marker

Tweezers or needle-nose pliers

Superfine steel wool (#0000)

80 grit sandpaper or round metalworking file

Sharp scissors

Butane lighter

Ruler

FINISHED SIZE

Approximately 23 inches

INSTRUCTIONS

Project note: *After cutting, melt ends of paracord using lighter. Materials and colors used are to aid in photography instructions and may not match finished project.*

1. Use steel wool to sand the copper tubing to a bright shine. **Note:** *Sand in the same directions as the length of the tubing and not across.*

2. Cut 14 (1-inch) pieces of copper tubing following the pipe cutter manufacturer's instructions. Roll a piece of 80 grit sandpaper to fit inside tubing. Insert sandpaper into tubing and sand to remove any rough edges. **Note:** *A round metalworking file may also be used to remove rough edges.*

3. Measure and mark 12 inches from end of one piece of cord. Tie an Overhand Knot (page 5) at mark. Pin knot to left side of cardboard.

4. Thread one prepared tube onto cord and slide up to knot (Figure 1).

Figure 1

5. Fold second cord in half. Insert folded end of cord into top of copper tube. Pin in place. Three cords should be coming out of the top of the tube, and one cord should be coming out of the bottom (Figure 2).

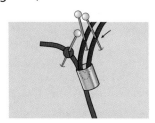

Figure 2

6. Thread the loose tail of cord from step 3 up into the bottom of tube, creating a loop. Wiggle the cords as needed to get them all into the tube. Now three cords will be coming out of the top of the tube, and two cords will be coming out the bottom of the tube (Figure 3).

Figure 3

7. Thread the top two cords down through a second copper tube. Thread the bottom two cords up through the second tube. ***Note:*** *Use a pair of tweezers or needle-nose pliers to reach*

down into the tube and pull the paracord through. Be careful not to damage or fray the cord. Keep the copper tubes about ⅝ inch apart. Adjust and re-pin as needed so cording arcs ½ inch above and below the tubes, and so tubes are parallel to each other (Figure 4).

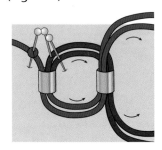

Figure 4

8. Repeat step 7 until five more tubes have been added.

9. To create your center focal point, adjust the arc of the cording to ¾ inch between tubes five and six. Adjust the arc of the cording to 1 inch between tubes six and seven. This will be your center focal point (Figure 5).

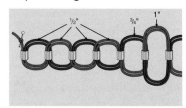

Figure 5

10. Repeat step 7 until five more tubes have been added, adjusting the arc between tubes seven and eight to ¾ inch and the arcs to ½ inch between the remaining four tubes. You should have 12 tubes on your cording (Figure 6).

Figure 6

11. Place a pin through the top two cords that go down through the last copper tube added. Pull out cords and trim ½ inch longer than pin marking. Melt ends and slide back into tube, adjusting arc as necessary (Figures 7a and 7b).

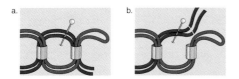

Figure 7

12. Place a pin through one cord right below tube 12. This is the cord that is looped, so pull one side out a few inches, trim ½ inch longer than pin, and melt end. Slide back into tube, adjusting the arc as necessary. The cord that remains through the top of the tube will be your necklace cord. Pull it all the way out of the final tube to its full length (Figures 8a and 8b).

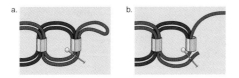

Figure 8

13. Move to a solid protected surface such as a work bench. Use a hammer to flatten each tube, removing pins as you flatten. Make sure cord ends are hidden within the tube before flattening.

14. Tie an Overhand Knot (page 5) just above tube 12 in the tail that sticks out the top.

15. Slide remaining, un-hammered tubes onto cord on each end of necklace. Tie an Overhand Knot, keeping knot close to tubing and tubing tight to knot below (Figure 9). ***Note:*** *If desired, stitch loops of center focal point together referring to main photo.*

Figure 9

16. Adjust end cords to desired necklace length, cut and melt ends. ***Note:*** *Project end cords are 4 inches.*

17. Sew copper clasp onto cord ends. ●

Earring Stash

Project note: *Only melt ends of paracord after cutting, using lighter when instructed to. Materials and colors used are to aid in photography instructions and may not match finished projects.*

COPPER & BLACK EARRINGS
(Make 2)

INSTRUCTIONS

1. String a copper compression sleeve and one jump ring onto a 5-inch piece of paracord. Fold paracord in half, bringing cut ends together. Use pliers to hold cord tightly together near cut ends. Melt two ends together using butane lighter. Use pliers to shape ends while nylon is hot so jump ring fits into melted area.

COPPER & BLACK EARRINGS MATERIALS
2 (5-inch) lengths black paracord with core removed
2 (¼-inch outer diameter) copper compression sleeves (sold in electrical supplies)
2 copper fishhook ear wires
2 (8mm) copper jump rings
Needle-nose pliers
Sharp scissors
Butane lighter
Ruler

FINISHED SIZE
2½ inches, including earring findings

2. After paracord has cooled, slide jump ring to top of earring. Open loop on ear wire and attach to jump ring. Close loop.

> *tip*
>
> Small pieces of paracord can be turned into earrings by pulling out the cores and then carefully melting the ends together.

ALL GEARED UP EARRINGS MATERIALS	Sharp scissors
	Butane lighter
Paracord with the core removed: 2 (3-inch) gray, 2 (1¼-inch) black	Ruler
	Needle-nose pliers
2 (¾-inch) metal gears or washers	**FINISHED SIZE**
2 silver or gunmetal ear wires	2¾ inches, including earring findings
2 (12mm) silver or gunmetal jump rings	

ALL GEARED UP EARRINGS
(Make 2)

INSTRUCTIONS

1. String gear onto 3-inch piece of gray paracord. Fold paracord in half, bringing cut ends together. Use pliers to hold cord tightly together near cut ends. Melt two ends together using butane lighter. Use pliers to shape ends while nylon is hot so jump ring fits into melted area.

2. Join ends on each black paracord piece to create a circle. (Hold the two pieces end to end with pliers and melt.) Slide black paracord over gray paracord from the top, melted end, down to just above the washer or gear.

3. Open jump ring and slide through paracord loop above black band. Slide on ear wire. Close jump ring.

CRYSTAL DISC EARRINGS
(Make 2)

INSTRUCTIONS

1. String a disc bead onto center of 10-inch paracord. Tie an Overhand Knot (page 5) just above the bead.

2. Trim ends 1 inch above knot. Use pliers to hold cords tightly together near ends.

CRYSTAL DISK EARRINGS MATERIALS	2 silver ear wires
	Sharp scissors
2 (10-inch) length blue w/dot paracord with core removed	Butane lighter
	Ruler
	Needle-nose pliers
2 (19mm) crystal disc beads	**FINISHED SIZE**
2 (12mm) silver jump rings	3 inches, including earring findings

Melt two ends together using butane lighter. Use pliers to shape ends while nylon is hot so jump ring fits into melted area.

3. Open jump ring and slide through paracord loop. Slide on ear wire. Close jump ring. ●

Project Gallery

31

33

37

41

39

44

Buyer's Guide

Due to the ever-changing nature of the bead industry, it may be impossible to find the exact beads and components used in the designs shown in this publication. Similar beads and components may be found via the Internet or by visiting your local bead shops and shows.

Bliss Beads Studio
(815) 517-0164
www.blissbeadstudio.com

Blue Moon Beads
(866) 404-7640
www.creativityinc.com

Darice Inc.
(866) 432-7423
www.darice.com

Fire Mountain Gems and Beads
(800) 423-2319
www.firemountaingems.com

Jesse James Beads
www.jessejamesbeads.com

Plaid
(800) 842-4197
www.plaidonline.com

The Buyer's Guide listings are provided as a service to our readers and should not be considered an endorsement from this publication.